THE LIFE & TIMES OF
LUDWIG VAN BEETHOVEN

THE LIFE & TIMES OF

Ludwig van Beethoven

BY
A. Noble

This edition printed for, Shooting Star Press Inc, 230
Fifth Avenue, Suite 1212, New York, NY 10001

Shooting Star Press books are available at special discount
for bulk purchases for sales promotions, premiums, fund-
raising or educational use. Special editions or book
excerpts can also be created to specification. For details
contact – Special Sales Director, Shooting Star Press Inc.,
230 Fifth Avenue, Suite 1212, New York, NY 10001

This edition first published by Parragon Books
Produced by Magpie Books Ltd, 7 Kensington Church
Court, London W8 4SP
Copyright © Parragon Book Service Ltd 1994
Cover picture & illustrations courtesy of: Mary Evans
Picture Library; Christies Images.

ISBN 1 57335 043 5
A copy of the British Library Cataloguing in Publication
Data is available from the British Library.

Typeset by Hewer Text Composition Services, Edinburgh
Printed in Singapore by Printlink International Co.

Childhood and Youth

The name Beethoven immediately conjures up the idea of the powerful, strong-willed, Romantic artist. The image of his brooding face, with its swept-back hair, its piercing eyes, its firm chin, matches the power of his music.

For Beethoven was a man with a mission: a mission to transform music. He viewed the artist as an independent soul, whose duty it was to set out his vision of the world, no matter who did or did not like it. The artist, in a sense, was the mouthpiece of God, and his genius was intrinsically right, in whatever it wanted to say. And without doubt, he achieved what he set out to do. By the time of his death he was revered as a Titan of music.

Ludwig van Beethoven was born on either 15 or 16 December 1770 (his family record was lost so we cannot be sure) into humble circumstances. Like Mozart, Beethoven had a musical father. Johann van Beethoven was a court musician in Bonn, the residence of the Elector of Cologne, whose archbishopric was one of the numerous petty principalities that made up Germany in the eighteenth century. Archbishop Maximilian Friedrich ran his court on a grand scale, employing numerous musicians and paying for many public entertainments.

Beethoven's musical ability apparently began to show at the age of five. At the age of seven he was sent to a Latin primary school where he was described as dirty and scruffy by one of his schoolmates – a description that was to be applied to him throughout his life. He stayed there for three or four years, before devoting his time fully to music. His father force-fed him with practice on the clavier and the violin. Not a day went without it. Finally, he performed publicly on 26 March 1778, billed as Johann's six-year-old son. For a long time Beethoven believed that he was born in 1772, and this was probably due to his father having falsified his age – as on this occasion – to make him appear more of an infant prodigy.

Over the next few years he was sent to a succession of teachers: to learn theory as well as singing and various instruments. One of his teachers remarked that he was a quiet and serious little boy and other sources state that he was very pensive. When he was thinking about music, and the feelings aroused by it, he was lost to the world. In 1781 he had lessons with the court organist Christian Gottlob Neefe, and in 1782 he was deputising for him at the organ. He apparently made great progress with Neefe, whose teaching skill he greatly respected. Also in 1782 he had his first Variations for piano published, based on a march by Dressler. He also was appointed as the unpaid 'cembalist' (harpsichord player) of the court orchestra. In October 1783 his 'Electoral' (because they were dedicated to the Elector) Sonatas were published, his first original work.

The following year the old Elector died, to be replaced by Maximilian Franz, who immediately set about reducing his predecessor's extravagance. Salaries were cut, including Neefe's and probably Beethoven's father's, but Beethoven himself received a salary of 150 florins, only fifty less than Neefe. At the same time Beethoven began giving piano lessons to members of the well-off von Breuning family to whom he had become very close. He needed the extra money as his mother was not well and his father was sinking into alcoholism. Teaching music to the von Breuning children was also of great benefit to Beethoven's own education; the von Breunings were very cultured, and introduced him to literature and poetry. They also encouraged him to attend the University of Bonn for philosophy lectures.

In April 1787, Beethoven visited Vienna where he stayed for several days. During this time he met Mozart, then working on *Don Giovanni*. Beethoven played something at Mozart's request; Mozart was not initially impressed as he assumed it was something he had practised. Beethoven then asked for a theme on which he could improvise, and this time Mozart was convinced of the young man's genius.

Beethoven's mother died in July 1787, which deeply affected him. His father was also falling into penury, having had to support a sick wife and sustain his drinking. This must have been burdensome to the young man. Fortunately however at about this time he met Count Waldstein (to whom the well-known Piano Sonata in C, Op. 53, would later be dedicated). Waldstein tactfully added to Beethoven's income from the Elector.

Throughout this period Beethoven continued to play in the court orchestra and to cultivate people of high social standing, and in 1789 he was recognized as head of the family, entitled to half his father's salary as well as his own. (His father had been dismissed from court service for being frequently drunk and disorderly.) He spent an increasing amount of time composing: two cantatas were written in 1790, as were many songs and some chamber music. He started to keep sketchbooks in which he set down ideas: these books indicate that he was planning a violin and an oboe concerto, as well as a symphony. By his twentieth year he was beginning to think on a grander scale.

Vienna

In the summer of 1791, Beethoven travelled
with Maximilian Franz's court to Mergen-
theim, for a gathering of the Teutonic
Knights of which Maximilian was master.
The spreading scale of Beethoven's reputa-
tion is shown by a contemporary report
which said that he surpassed many of his
contemporaries as he was an equally great
pianist as an *adagio* or *allegro* player. In other
words, he was equally expressive in slower,
more thoughtful music as in happy music.

The report also stated that the whole orchestra admired him, always the greatest accolade.

Haydn visited Bonn the following year, and it is believed that he met Beethoven on this occasion. In October, Beethoven was still playing in the court orchestra. Then, and the details are unknown, he was sent at the Elector's expense to Vienna to study under Haydn. The date of his departure was 2 November 1792, and he had a hair-raising trip, having to pass through the Hessian army and nearly running into the French en route (France was at war with most of Europe at this time, after the French Revolution). He would never see Bonn again.

Beethoven's life was typical of that of the poor student: he kept scrupulous accounts of his expenditure which give evidence of how small his income was. Haydn even wrote to the Elector to ask that his allowance be increased, sending some of his pupil's compositions to sugar the pill. Haydn also wanted to be repaid some money he had lent Beethoven. The response was hardly what he expected: the Elector said that Beethoven did not seem to be making enough progress in his composition, and suggested that he return to Bonn! Three months later he actually cut off Beethoven's allowance. Haydn had been going to take Beethoven to London in 1794 but, as Beethoven was near penniless, had to depart without him.

Study continued, however, under the violinist Ignaz Schuppanzigh, Johann Albrechtsberger, a master of counterpoint, and under Antonio Salieri, Mozart's erstwhile rival, who was prepared to give impecunious students lessons in opera composition for free. Meanwhile, Beethoven gave piano concerts, often improvising ingeniously and brilliantly, to the dismay of his competitors. He even had to start writing down his variations as they were plagiarised wholesale.

He also became more intimate with the cultured aristocracy; the artist was coming to be recognised as an equal rather than as a servant as had been the case for Haydn. Two important figures in his circle were Baron Gottfried van Swieten (who had been a supporter of Mozart) and Prince Karl Lichnowsky (who had been one of Mozart's pupils as well). Lichnowsky's brother-in-law, Count Rasumovsky, was another patron who would later have the Quartets, Op. 59, dedicated to him. Beethoven made no attempt to flatter his patrons, either by taking

Young Beethoven

Beethoven improvises for Mozart

care of his appearance – he was generally ill-kempt – or being amenable to their desires. One report has him lounging on a sofa refusing to play for Lichnowsky's mother when he did not feel like it.

It was at Lichnowsky's that Beethoven played his Op. 1 Piano Trios, prior to their being published by Artaria in 1795. The audience was highly distinguished, and included Haydn. He approved of the works apart from the third, and this led to Beethoven resenting Haydn – he was always quick to anger. He had already been arrogant with regard to the great composer by refusing to describe himself as one of Haydn's pupils on published work, asserting that he had learnt nothing from him. The works on publication sold 241 copies and Beethoven made a substantial sum out of them.

The Napoleonic wars, and the massive dislocation they caused, meant that Vienna became more of a home from home for Beethoven, as many refugees arrived from Germany. His brother Caspar arrived in June 1794, and other friends fled the French occupation of Bonn. Beethoven formally made his debut in Vienna on 29 March 1795, at a benefit concert. He played his new Piano Concerto in B flat, No. 2, Op. 19. This was actually his first concerto written as an adult but because it was not published until after the concerto in C, Op. 15, in December 1801, it is known as the second. The orchestra must have been large, as 150 participants are recorded. Eye-witnesses described Beethoven's playing as very powerful, even causing audiences to weep with emotion. But often when he had caused such an effect he simply laughed at their

sentimentality! In May he signed a contract
with Artaria, and as well as studying he was
constantly in demand to perform and com-
pose. He received the honour of a commission in 1795 for the annual masked ball,
which put him in the company of masters
such as Dittersdorf, Haydn and the Imperial
Kapellmeister Sussmayr (Mozart's old pupil).
He also collaborated with Haydn in two
concerts at the end of the year, which
implied that their differences had been
resolved.

The new year, 1796, saw him in a good
position: his Op. 2 Sonatas, dedicated to
Haydn, were published in March. He
clearly earned a good income, having a
servant, a horse and his own apartment
(though he was so absent-minded that he
forgot about the horse, which his servant

secretly rented out to make money on the side). His friends included many artists and members of the aristocracy. He went on a tour in 1796 that included Prague, Dresden, Leipzig and Berlin between February and July. In Berlin he received a gold snuffbox full of money, a present which Beethoven described as one fitting for an ambassador. Back in Vienna he still gave lessons, apparently visiting one pupil who lived opposite him in his dressing gown, nightcap and slippers, which was regarded as highly eccentric if typical of Beethoven.

In 1797 the Op. 5 Cello Sonatas were published, No. 1 in F major and No. 2 in G minor. These works remain among his best-loved. They were followed by the Quintet in E flat major for piano and wind instruments, Op. 16. This is an unusual work, as usually the piano would be accompanied by strings: here they are replaced by clarinet, oboe, horn and bassoon. The idea of using this instrumentation is based on Mozart's quintet (K. 452). The tone colours are very effective and the work does not deserve its comparative neglect. It was performed frequently at the time to great applause.

In 1798 Beethoven was introduced to Jean Baptiste Bernadotte, the French general who was later to become King of Sweden, but who was currently ambassador to Austria. It was he who suggested a 'Heroic' symphony, which was to become the 'Eroica' (Symphony No. 3 in E flat, Op. 55). At the end of this year Beethoven also returned to Prague to perform his new C major piano concerto, Op. 15, now known as No. 1, and the revised Op. 19. Already he was noted for the sombre and mysterious nature of his playing, and his new methods of developing ideas that ignored previous musical logic. He also began to stress the importance of originality, feigning not to know Mozart's operas because they might influence him!

At the end of 1799 Beethoven completed a work that is familiar to us all: the Piano Sonata in C minor, Op. 13, the 'Pathétique', dedicated to Lichnowsky. Many have seen this work as the one which broke with eighteenth century Classicism, heralding the new age of Romanticism.

Sonata Opus 26

Beethoven with his pupil Teresa Brunswick

In early 1800 Beethoven gave his first sub-
scription concert for his own benefit. It
included works by Haydn and Mozart but
also it premiered Beethoven's First Symphony, in C, Op. 21, and his Septet in E flat
major, Op. 20. Unfortunately, the playing of
the orchestra was extremely scrappy and
failed to do justice to the symphony. It
only became popular after publication in
December 1801. But the Septet was an
instant hit. It is a pleasant, sunny work,
similar in some respects to Schubert's Oc-
tet, and is still popular. Beethoven, however,
was apparently furious at its immediate and
lasting success, because he had vested his
hopes in the First Symphony.

1801 was a busy year starting with public
concerts for the benefit of soldiers wounded
at the battle of Hohenlinden, and then a

performance of Beethoven's first stage work (if one excludes the adolescent *Ritterballet*), the *Prometheus* ballet, written in collaboration with Salvatore Vigano, the imperial ballet master. It was a success, receiving over 29 performances in 1801 and 1802, with the piano arrangement being published in June 1801.

It is from 1801, too, that Beethoven's correspondence has survived in significant quantities and gives us an insight into his views on several matters. His advances in style were not universally admired by the music critics, and he wrote to the publisher of one music paper that they should be less damning of new works – not for himself, he could cope with it – but in case they put off other able new composers. He also wrote about his health, which had never been that good, with constant chronic stomach problems, and in a letter written on 29 June 1802 he complains of his increasing deafness. None of the doctors he saw were able to ease this latter problem, and it must have been incredibly depressing for a musician to suffer from this disability. He had to sit close to the orchestra to hear what was being played, and could not hear high notes at any distance. Socially, it was a disaster too. He was unable to hear if people spoke softly – his only escape was to pretend it was due to his well-known absent-mindedness – yet it physically hurt him if people shouted.

The depression caused by his deafness came to a head when he was taking a summer vacation in the village of Heiligenstadt, on the recommendation of his doctor. Walking with his pupil, Ferdinand Ries, he was totally unable to hear a shepherd on his flute. He sank into deep gloom and, in this mood, on 6 October he wrote to his brothers Carl and Johann. In his letter he says the world was wrong to see him as a recluse. He had first suffered loss of hearing in 1796, and its gradual worsening had forced him to cut himself off from the world; 'Though endowed with a passionate and lively temperament and even fond of the distractions offered by society, I was soon obliged to seclude myself and live in solitude.' If he ever tried to ignore his deafness, it would always 'humiliate' him when with others. He keenly felt that in his profession his hearing should be superior to that of most people – as indeed it had once been. He had even contemplated suicide: the thoughts that prevented him were a desire to complete the compositions he knew he had in him, and a sustaining philosophy. With this letter, known as the Heiligenstadt Testament, he effectively made his farewell to society. His life now would be purely dedicated to his art, with no distraction.

Back in Vienna, Beethoven threw himself into composition, as if liberated by his decision to retire from the world socially. The Second Symphony, in D, Op. 36, was the immediate result. This work is surprisingly cheerful, given his acute feelings of depression. With it, Beethoven left the legacy of Mozart and Haydn behind. It is broadly experimental, exploring new ideas with vigour, much grander than previous works. It has humour and breadth, and is in many ways the first Romantic symphony. It caused such excitement when first performed that young people were warned not to listen to it, as it might cause 'moral corruption'. He also wrote the three Piano Sonatas Op. 31, No. 16 in G major, No. 17 in D major (the 'Tempest' Sonata) and No. 18 in E flat, and the three Violin Sonatas Op. 30, No. 1 in A major, No. 2 in C minor and No. 3 in G major. These works are generally regarded as marking the beginning of Beethoven's second period, a period in which his musical individuality becomes more pronounced and in which he would mark out for himself the path he would follow.

For Schikaneder's Theater an der Wien he wrote the oratorio *Christus am Ölberg* (Christ on the Mount of Olives) which was performed together with his recently 'finished' Third Piano Concerto in C minor, Op. 37. Apparently, the man who turned the pages for Beethoven during the premiere of the Piano

Advertisement showing head of Beethoven

Illustration to the 'Moonlight Sonata'

Concerto described his writing as hiero-glyphs, serving as a sort of code for Beetho-ven, who essentially played the solo part from memory. The concert was not a great success; rehearsals had not gone well and *Christus* was felt to be too long and superficial, despite some good passages. Nonetheless Beethoven received 1800 florins and was commissioned to write an opera. On 24 May a rather more successful concert was given, featuring the Violin Sonata in A, Op. 47 'Kreutzer'. The two instruments work together in a novel way, with neither subordinate to the other. The sonata was dedicated to Rodolphe Kreutzer, a famous French violinist and composer, apparently after Beethoven had argued with the original dedicatee over a woman. Kreutzer himself declared it 'out-rageously unintelligible' when he saw it!

In the summer Beethoven went to Öberdö-
bling where he spent the entire season
composing the symphony that would become the 'Eroica' in E flat, Op. 55. This
symphony was scored for the largest orchestra used up to that time and in terms of
power, and the piling up of themes, the
shifting from key to key, and the many
sudden climaxes, it must have confused its
original listeners. The second movement
funeral march is very moving and is perhaps
the best-known part of the symphony. The
march may have been written to commem-
orate Beethoven's disillusionment at the
behaviour of Napoleon Bonaparte. Ries
commented that he had come into Beethoven's room to find a blank piece of paper
with 'Buonaparte' at the top and 'Luigi van
Beethoven' at the bottom. Beethoven had
particularly admired Napoleon's conduct as

First Consul, enacting new laws and bringing some stability to republican France. When he heard that Napoleon had declared himself Emperor, he lost his temper, shouting, 'Is he then nothing but an ordinary human? Now he will trample the rights of men underfoot and serve only his own ambition . . he will become a tyrant.' Immediately he tore up the title page and renamed the symphony the *Sinfonia Eroica.* When published in October 1806, it bore the words 'To the memory of a great man'.

In 1804 Beethoven also completed the Triple Concerto for piano, violin and cello, Op. 56, and the Piano Sonata in C major, Op. 53, 'Waldstein'. The latter, from its opening repetitive chords, is a very powerful piece of music and is still popular at concerts. He also wrote the Piano Sonata in F minor, Op. 57, 'Appassionata', which apparently he composed in his head on a walk with Ries. Interestingly, he had received a new piano from Erard, the French manufacturer, which featured an extended range, enabling greater flexibility in composition. (The piano developed substantially during the late eighteenth century and during the nineteenth, towards the end of which it reached modern levels of power and range; originally it had been quite a soft-toned feeble instrument, unable to dominate an orchestra; this affected writing for it as it could only be heard when the orchestra was silent or playing softly.) He also began to work on the opera *Fidelio*. The *Prometheus* Overture, Op. 43 (first performed in 1801), the Second Symphony and the Third Piano Concerto were also published. By the end of 1804 he was famous throughout Europe: as

one writer, Thayer, put it, he was 'a recognised member of the great triumvirate,
Haydn, Mozart and Beethoven', a position
in which he has remained ever since.

The Spirit in Command

The 'Eroica', conducted by Beethoven himself, received its first public performance on 7 April 1805 at the Theater an der Wien. Critics were taken aback: it was full of energy and novelty, and one found it a 'daring and wild fantasia'. For a start it was longer than any symphonies they had heard before, and they found it hard to keep track as it developed, leaping from one mood to another. Previous music, including much of Beethoven's, had been more compartmentalised. The audience could quickly settle into the mood of a movement and expect no surprises. This had now changed and it divided his following: some thought that his genius brooked no carping, that audiences were not sophisticated enough to understand him; some thought he strove after originality and unusual effects for their own sake rather than for the creation of beauty; and some felt that there were beautiful parts to the music but yearned for a return to a simpler past.

The most important development of 1805, however, was the completion of *Fidelio*, which Beethoven had been working on for over a year. (There are three *Leonore* – the working title for the opera – overtures, which were superseded by the final version.) The libretto, by Joseph Sonnleithner was adapted from J. N. Bouilly's *Léonore ou l'amour conjugal* (Leonore, or conjugal love). Bouilly's story was based on a true incident during the Terror in France, where a devoted wife managed to save her imprisoned husband from the guillotine. His story was immediately popular and several other composers based operas on it, some of which Beethoven knew. Because of political difficulties – there were French soldiers from the army of occupation in the theatre when it was first performed – Sonnleithner changed the setting from France to Spain. The hero is Florestan, a fighter for freedom, held in prison by the Governor Don Pizarro. Leonore, disguised as the boy Fidelio, becomes assistant to the gaoler Rocco. Pizarro has decided to kill Florestan and tries to bribe Rocco to do the dirty deed. Rocco, after some doubts, refuses, but agrees to dig the grave. Pizarro is only prevented from killing

Florestan by the intervention of Leonore with a pistol. At this point, trumpets announce the arrival of Don Fernando, a government minister. Pizarro is arrested and the prisoners, including Florestan, are released. Beethoven was always very involved in the project as Leonore represented for him the embodiment of Romantic ideals.

The opera was essentially a *Singspiel*, with dialogue interspersed with music. The premiere was on 20 November. Unfortunately as Sonnleithner's libretto was so badly constructed, and Beethoven's operatic experience was so limited, it was not a success, and was taken off after three performances. Beethoven was furious: he had worked on *Fidelio* for nearly two years. When it was suggested afterwards at a meeting at Lichnowsky's house that he alter the score and make cuts he refused point blank – 'Not one note'. Eventually he succumbed to Princess Lichnowsky begging him, literally on her knees, to do so, and he relented. His friend Stephan von Breuning revised the libretto, cutting it from three to two acts, and Beethoven worked on the score. When it was presented again, a year later, it was, if anything, less successful, receiving only two performances. Beethoven was very upset by this second rejection and began to refer to the opera as his 'crown of martyrdom'. It had to wait until 1814 for a full revision.

To put its poor reception into context, however, the French had just defeated the Austrian and Russian armies, arriving in Vienna on 13 November, causing pandemonium amongst the population. The bet-

Beethoven composing a symphony

Romantic landscape in winter

between the sombre grandeur of the 'Eroica' and the drama of the Fifth. It is lighter and more vivacious in tone, and has less of the overt passion of the two symphonies to either side of it. Robert Schumann described it as a 'Grecian maiden between two Nordic giants'. The stay with Lichnowsky came to an abrupt end when Lichnowsky promised some French occupying officers that Beethoven would play for them. As might be imagined this did not go down well and Beethoven refused, packing his bags immediately and heading off through pouring rain to stay at a friend's. Unfortunately this walk in the rain aggravated his deafness.

The Fourth Piano Concerto in G, Op. 58, was also completed during this period. This work has remained a favourite in the repertoire ever since. It is very lyrical and serenely joyful – in many ways sharing the mood of the Fourth Symphony. The most striking innovation, perhaps, was the opening of the concerto with the piano solo for a few bars, rather than the usual orchestral tutti. Mozart had used this approach once but only in an early work. Beethoven also composed the Violin Concerto in D, Op. 61. He had contemplated writing a violin concerto for many years, and had set down sketches for such a work but nothing had come of them. The concerto was commissioned by the violinist Franz Clement, for a concert for his benefit on 23 December 1806. Clement worked with the composer to resolve technical difficulties that arose in the violin part. The work was finished very quickly and in some respects is less innovatory than his other works. It is also rather loosely constructed and requires that the soloist be a

Portrait of the older Beethoven

Illustration to *Fidelio*

sensitive as well as proficient musician. As was commented at the time it had 'originality and numerous beautiful passages . . . [but some] connoisseurs . . . recognise that the musical argument is often quite loose and the endless repetition of rather mundane passages might become wearisome.'

In April 1807 Beethoven signed a contract with the London music publisher, Muzio Clementi, handing over several manuscripts, some of which Clementi would have adapted (e.g. the Violin Concerto rewritten for piano), and the promise of two sonatas and a fantasia for the piano. In all he was paid £260 for these works, a considerable sum. He spent the summer at Baden and Heiligenstadt, working on the Fifth Symphony in C minor, Op. 67, and the Mass in C, Op. 86, commissioned by Prince Nikolaus Esterhazy.

Of the opening bars of the Fifth, Beethoven reputedly said: 'Thus Fate knocks on the door.' This dramatic statement is born out in the music, which wears its emotional heart on its sleeve. The rhythm of the opening bars dominates the first movement; in a sense they are simple, but Beethoven managed to generate a potent and beautiful impression from only three tones in the scale. In the second movement the two principal melodies are supported by great harmonic richness. The symphony is exciting and affecting, Olympian in its effect.

Towards the end of 1807 there were a series of concerts featuring Beethoven's music, and these were regarded as crowd-pullers, contrary to the myth that his work was rarely performed in Vienna. It is true that not all of his work was received without criticism, as

has been noted, but his music clearly fasci-
nated as well as frightened.

In 1808 Beethoven devoted himself to the
completion of the Fifth Symphony and the
Sixth, in F, Op. 68, 'Pastoral'. They were
premiered on 22 December 1808, together
with the Fourth Piano Concerto and the
rather unusual 'Choral' Fantasia in C minor,
Op. 80, for piano, chorus and orchestra, also
composed in 1808. The Sixth is regarded, as
its title implies, as programme music, that is
music intended to depict specific scenes; the
headings for the movements support this: I
Happy feelings on arrival in the country; II
By the brook; III Peasant merrymaking; IV
The storm; and V Shepherds' song – relief
and pleasure at the passing of the storm.
Beethoven wanted to evoke a general feel-
ing rather than be too specifically program-

matic; his success can be inferred from the fact that one does not find the programme distracting one from the music. Strangely enough, at the time, the Fifth Symphony was seen as more programmatic than the Sixth, often being known as the 'Fate' Symphony. Its impact was described by E. T. A. Hoffmann, the Romantic musician and story writer. Haydn, he said, was 'youthful and lighthearted' in his music, Mozart led one into a spiritual world, whereas 'Beethoven's instrumental music opens up to us the world of the immense and infinite'. He also perhaps identified why Beethoven was not so successful as a vocal composer, because the use of words to some extent defines the meaning of the music to the listener and thereby denies full freedom to the emotional response. The concert was well received, but Beethoven had grown tired of the squabbling that surrounded the promotion of concerts – Salieri was named as being particularly troublesome – and of the adverse reviews that were published despite the popular acclaim. And so 22 December 1808 was his last public appearance as a solo pianist.

In the autumn he had been offered a position by King Jerome of Westphalia (Napoleon's brother) and had been sorely tempted to take it, as a means of escaping the malicious intrigues of Vienna. His friends were aghast and the Countess Maria Erdödy, with whom Beethoven seems to have had one of his many affairs, launched a campaign to keep him there, persuading several members of the aristocracy to band together and draw up a contract that would persuade Beethoven to stay. Beethoven was quite demanding: he stated that an artist should be in a position to work free from financial worry; he asked for more money than King Jerome had been prepared to offer; and he wanted to be guaranteed a concert every Palm Sunday at the Theater an der Wien for his personal benefit, at which 'new and greater works' would be performed. His wishes were granted and the contract was drawn up on 1 March 1809. The sponsors were the Archduke Rudolf, Prince Lokbowitz and Prince Ferdinand Kinsky.

On the night of 11 May 1809 the French again besieged and bombarded Vienna. The Imperial Family had already left. Beethoven hid in a cellar with pillows over his head. The following day the city capitulated. The French reoccupied the town and the atmosphere grew oppressive, with the conquerors impos-

Beethoven's house in Bonn

Illustration to the Ninth Symphony

ing heavy taxes on the Viennese. They also blew up the city walls which were right next to Beethoven's lodgings. Inflation was rampant and many people were reduced to poverty. The Emperor did not return until November when peace negotiations were under way.

Even in these difficult times, and his health was poor as well, Beethoven managed to complete several works: the Fifth Piano Concerto in E flat minor, 'The Emperor', Op. 73, the String Quartet in E flat, Op. 74, some songs and several piano sonatas. Publications included the Cello Sonata in A major, Op. 69, and the Op. 70 Piano Trios, of which No. 1, in D major, (dedicated to Countess Erdödy). is the well-known 'Ghost' Trio, so called because of the rather mysterious music of the second movement Ironically though, despite now having financial security, he was to produce very little over the next ten years, much to the disappointment of his sponsors.

In October 1809 he began work on the *Egmont* overture, to be performed with Goethe's play of that name. It was completed the following June. This is a very powerful work, strikingly stark, and reflects Beethoven's admiration for the poet, and for the subject matter, an individual fighting oppression. In 1810, too, he completed the String Quartet in F minor, Op. 95. This quartet reflects some of the unhappiness he felt at the time. He had proposed to Therese von Brunswick and been rejected, and he seems to have felt that this would be his last chance to marry. The quartet is very dense, more so in its opening *allegro* than the great late quartets, full of lyrical ideas expressed extremely briefly, with many sudden key changes. 1811 was mostly spent working on the proofs for his many publications. He was constantly irritated by the incompetence of the publishers. Nonetheless he was cheerful enough to pen the Piano Trio in B flat, Op. 97, 'Archduke', in three weeks flat. Deservedly this is Beethoven's most popular trio. From its gentle opening bars onwards it radiates a serene happiness.

He also received a commission to write the overtures to *King Stephen* and *The Ruins of Athens*, two plays that were to inaugurate a new theatre in Pest, and completed the work during his summer visit to the spa at Teplitz. He began sketches for two more symphonies, the Seventh in A, Op. 92, and the Eighth in F, Op. 93. These were completed in May and October 1812. Concert life in general was flat in 1811. To pay for the war the government had massively devalued the currency, effectively reducing Beethoven's stipend from 4,000 gulden a year to 1600. Nonetheless he managed to spend the summer in various spas.

In 1812 he finally met his hero Goethe at Teplitz. Goethe wrote that 'His talent amazed me; unfortunately he is an utterly untamed personality . . . not altogether wrong in detesting the world.' Goethe sympathised with Beethoven because of his deafness, which he recognised as the most painful disability a musician could have. His playing had obviously suffered: his *fortissimi* were now almost too loud, and his *pianissimi* so quiet that audiences could barely hear them. But little of his distress showed in his two latest symphonies. The Seventh is a particularly optimistic work, vigorous and world-affirming, with a solemn and sublime second movement, beginning like a second funeral march (compare the 'Eroica') that resolves itself into a hymn of joy. The last movement, perhaps somewhat 'tub-thumping' as the great conductor Sir Thomas Beecham might have said, has an elemental force, being almost a cosmic dance, punctuated with brisk, militaristic brass. The Eighth is a much shorter work, launching straight into its first theme without preamble. Though there is occasional dark orchestral shading, the emotions it expresses seem straightforward after the Seventh. The second movement is humorous, jolly even, and the third exudes cheerful contentment.

Beethoven's financial and family difficulties increased in 1813. He had to find money to support his ailing brother Carl, eventually borrowing it from one of his publishers. He also had had a major row with his brother Johann over the woman Johann wanted to, and did marry. Breitkopf and Härtel, another of his publishers, ceased to do business with him; Prince Kinsky had died at the end of 1812 and his annuity ceased, and Prince Lobkowitz failed to pay up – eventually Beethoven resorted to suing him. His fortunes only revived towards the end of the year when with Johann Mälzel he put on a benefit concert for Austrian soldiers wounded at the Battle of Hanau. The occasion for the concert was Wellington's crushing victory over the French at Vittoria in the summer, welcome news to the Austrians. Mälzel persuaded Beethoven to write his 'Battle' Symphony; Mälzel was a prolific inventor (he produced the metronome in

The lonely hunter

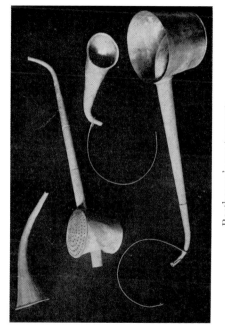

Beethoven's ear trumpets

1815) and had produced a machine called the panharmonicon (i.e. all harmony machine) which could reproduce the sound of an orchestra, and it was for this that the symphony was written. So on 8 December 1813, the concert took place in the Great Hall of Vienna University. The Seventh Symphony was also to receive its first public performance. The concert's success was resounding; the second movement of the Seventh Symphony had to be repeated, so rapturous was the applause – and the whole concert had to be repeated the following Sunday. A considerable sum of money was raised, and with this concert Beethoven achieved the popular acclaim that had so far eluded him.

Beethoven had agreed with Mälzel that they would share any profits made from future performances of the 'Battle' Symphony but, as was so often the case in his business and personal relationships – he was increasingly curmudgeonly – fell out with the inventor. In January 1814 Beethoven kept all the receipts from a benefit concert to himself; the symphony, if anything, increased in popularity and was clearly a money spinner. Mälzel tried to put on a performance in London: Beethoven not only wrote to the 'Musicians of London' asking them to boycott this, he also sued Mälzel. The lawsuit went on for three years, until Mälzel returned to Vienna and the two made up. It demonstrates the extreme lengths to which Beethoven was prepared to go to satisfy his bilious nature.

The new year went well with many concerts and, very pleasing to Beethoven, a request from three well-known singers, that *Fidelio*

Bronze bust of Beethoven

Unveiling of the Beethoven memorial in Bonn

Giant of Music

Between this period, when he had effectively established himself as *the* leading composer, and his death, Beethoven moved into totally new musical territory. It was not just that the musical forces he had employed were greater than any of his predecessors – the orchestras he required for his symphonies had grown to twice the size – he also took the piano sonata and the string quartet on to a new plane. Not only are they much longer than previously, they make extensive and unusual use of counterpoint, with different themes running virtually simultaneously, and of the fugue. Beethoven was a great admirer of his Baroque forebears, Handel and Bach – Handel he regarded as the greatest of all composers, and Bach the master of harmony – and it had been they who had truly developed these two musical modes that Beethoven was to use so adeptly.

The pieces that stand out in this period are: the last five piano sonatas, the Diabelli Variations, the *Missa Solemnis*, the Ninth Symphony and the last five string quartets. Plans for much other music, including more operas, existed (indeed, the Tenth Symphony has recently been completed from the sketches and performed). Diabelli worked at Beethoven's publishers – Steiner – and wanted to put together a collection of variations by different composers, including Hummel, Liszt and Schubert, on one of his own waltzes. To everyone's surprise, including his own, considering the feebleness of the original theme, Beethoven responded by writing an ever-increasing number of variations himself – first six or seven, then nine, then twenty-five and finally thirty-three. In announcing their publication, Diabelli did not mince his words: '. . . a great and important masterpiece . . . such as only Beethoven, the greatest living representative of true art . . . can produce. The most original structures and ideas, the boldest musical idioms and harmonies are exhausted . . .' A verdict that has been endorsed by music critics since.

The composition of the Diabelli Variations took place during the period 1819-23, during which Beethoven also worked on the *Missa Solemnis*. This was composed for the Archduke Rudolf's coronation as Archbishop of Olmütz in Moravia, to take place in Cologne on 20 March 1820. Rudolf had been one of Beethoven's better pupils, they were friends and Rudolf had since sponsored his old teacher, and Beethoven in turn had dedicated many of his works to him (witness the Archduke Trio). Beethoven chose the key of D major, with its connotations of happiness and dignity (it had been the key of Bach's B minor Mass – despite the title – and was also the key of the 'Ode to Joy' in the Ninth Symphony). He took immense pains over the work – having the text of the mass translated into German so that he could observe every nuance of meaning – and each movement grew as he wrote it. He researched the work of Palestrina, whom he regarded as a great church composer. In the event, he completely missed the deadline, not completing it until early 1823. It is a monumental work, a gigantic choral symphony, in which the vocal soloists are dwarfed by colossal orchestral forces, where man is but an atom in the face of the Creator. It radiates sincere belief – the heading of the first movement is 'vom Herzen' (from the heart). It ranks with such works as Verdi's *Requiem*.

Immediately it was completed, Beethoven showed that other facet of his character – the rather dubious businessman. He offered it to no less than seven different publishers, settling for the highest bidder, Schott, who paid 1000 gulden. He also engaged in financial shenanigans with the Philharmonic Society in London. They had always strongly favoured Beethoven, including much of his music in their concerts. In 1815 they offered him 75 guineas (£78.75) for three new overtures, and received *The Ruins of Athens*, *King Stephien* and *Namensfeier*, which were neither new nor particularly inspired. When they complained, Beethoven replied that they had been quite well received elsewhere, and the problem was that they had not been played properly! Amazingly, the Society still continued to treat with Beethoven and in 1816 offered 300 guineas (£375) for two new symphonies, and invited him to London. Beethoven tried to screw more money out of the Society, claiming extra travelling expenses and the need to hire a companion. Negotiations dragged on before petering out with neither party giving ground. They revived in July 1822, when the

Philharmonic Society made an offer of
£50 for a 'grand symphony'. This symphony was the Ninth in D minor, Op. 125,
completed over a year late, in early 1824.
Originally it was inscribed as being 'written
for the Philharmonic Society', which natu-
rally gave the Society the idea that it had
right of first performance. In the event,
however, not only was it performed twice
in Vienna (first played on 24 May 1824),
before the London premiere in March
1825, but the dedication on the published
version was to the King of Prussia! The
Society was very forgiving nonetheless and
in 1827 sent Beethoven an advance of £100
for a concert.

The gestation period of the Ninth Symphony was extremely long: Beethoven had
first had the idea of setting Schiller's *An*

die Freude (*Ode to Joy*) in the early 1790s. He mentions that he would be writing the Ninth in 1812 and sketches exist from 1815, with D minor being the chosen key and the idea of including voices already established. He found it very difficult to plan, unlike for his other symphonies, discarding many ideas, and uncertain how to proceed, not knowing when to bring in voices, in the second, third or last movement. It was probably the £50 of the Philharmonic Society that spurred him into completing it. The symphony uses even larger forces than those that had preceded it, including a chorus and soloists. The questioning hesitancy of the opening bars intermingles during the first movement with assertive tuttis, later mutating into a mysterious theme that develops into music of great confidence. Brahms was heavily influenced by it. The second movement has a bustling quality, with very short phrasing, constantly switching from fidgety strings to the woodwind and brass. It closes with a weighty prefiguring of the choral movement. The third movement is a serene interlude; the strings dominate, pensive and reflective. Towards the close of the movement the horns burst out, before the theme of tranquillity reasserts itself. The last movement opens ominously, with trumpets and drums almost suggesting a day of judgement, and the strings, in unison, acting almost as one giant instrument. Shortly afterwards the well-known theme to the *Ode to Joy* makes its first tentative appearance, is suppressed, and then reappears quietly and simply – almost harking back to the preceding movement. It grows in confidence and power as more of the orchestra, trumpets and drums come into play. The excitement mounts, only to be broken briefly, before the first voice, a bass, breaks in and begins to declaim the verse. Other voices come in, and all ends in a triumphant climax.

The first performance was not that successful: the symphony had only received two rehearsals and many of the musicians had no idea of how they were supposed to play it; the theatre was half-full and the profit was small (420 florins). But such audience as there was cheered at the end, throwing up their hats and waving their handkerchiefs. Beethoven, facing the orchestra, was unaware of this reception, being totally deaf, and had to be turned round by one of the soloists; when he bowed in acknowledgement, the response was rapturous. But afterwards, Beethoven was more concerned with the receipts and accused the theatre manager and others of cheating him, including Anton Schindler, one of his first biographers. Schindler was accused in a letter of being dishonest and unwelcome at Beethoven's table. This breach was not patched over until the end of 1826, and is typical of Beethoven's relations with those who were close to him – explosive, easily suspicious and vindictive, with grievances usually expressed in a superior, if hurt, moral tone.

Beethoven's health had been steadily worsening. His deafness had been complete since 1815, which had made him increasingly introverted and anti-social. He was assailed by other illnesses – rheumatism, catarrh and heart strain. He had jaundice in 1821 and an eye condition between April 1823 and January 1824 that meant he could not bear bright light. Finally towards the end of 1826 he contracted dropsy, an illness in which the body accumulates water in the tissue due to failure in the renal system. After four months of acute pain he died on 26 March 1827. The weather was brooding and sullen. As he lay dying, according to one witness there was a loud clap of thunder, and Beethoven 'opened his eyes, raised his right hand, and, his fist clenched, looked upwards for several seconds' before sliding out of life. An appropriate end for one of the giants of the Romantic era.

He was buried on 29 March: enormous crowds attended the funeral and over two hundred carriages accompanied the cortège to the cemetery. The crush was so dense outside the church where the funeral service was held that many fainted and had to be carried to a hospital opposite. The day was fine and warm; it was as if the Immortals wished to give Beethoven a fitting welcome to their company.

LIFE AND TIMES

Julius Caesar
Hitler
Monet
Van Gogh
Beethoven
Mozart
Mother Teresa
Florence Nightingale
Anne Frank
Napoleon

LIFE AND TIMES

JFK
Martin Luther King
Marco Polo
Christopher Columbus
Stalin
William Shakespeare
Oscar Wilde
Castro
Gandhi
Einstein

FURTHER MINI SERIES
INCLUDE

ILLUSTRATED POETS

Robert Burns
Shakespeare
Oscar Wilde
Emily Dickinson
Christina Rossetti
Shakespeare's Love Sonnets

FURTHER MINI SERIES INCLUDE

HEROES OF THE WILD WEST

General Custer
Butch Cassidy and the Sundance Kid
Billy the Kid
Annie Oakley
Buffalo Bill
Geronimo
Wyatt Earp
Doc Holliday
Sitting Bull
Jesse James

FURTHER MINI SERIES INCLUDE

THEY DIED TOO YOUNG

Elvis
James Dean
Buddy Holly
Jimi Hendrix
Sid Vicious
Marc Bolan
Ayrton Senna
Marilyn Monroe
Jim Morrison

THEY DIED TOO YOUNG

Malcolm X
Kurt Cobain
River Phoenix
John Lennon
Glenn Miller
Isadora Duncan
Rudolph Valentino
Freddie Mercury
Bob Marley